Zen Litter Box
GARDENING

T0364074

Running Press
Hachette Book Group
1290 Avenue of the Americas, New York, NY 10104
www.runningpress.com
@Running_Press

First Edition: March 2019

Published by Running Press, an imprint of Perseus Books, LLC,
a subsidiary of Hachette Book Group, Inc. The Running Press
name and logo is a trademark of the Hachette Book Group.

The publisher is not responsible for websites (or their content)
that are not owned by the publisher.

ISBN: 978-0-7624-6412-8

Contents

OPENING
THE BOX

There are many paths to enlightenment. Be sure to take one with a cat.

—*Lao Tzu*

It's amazing how cats can so perfectly encapsulate Zen meditation.

One need only watch a cat for a few moments to understand this. Cats do one thing at a time, and deliberately and utterly live in the moment. They pause. They observe. They respond.

Cats are the most popular pet in America, much to the chagrin of canine lovers. Cat brains are 90 percent similar to human beings—though cats do *much* better in the relaxation realm, sleeping 70 percent of their lives. While owning a cat has been proven to reduce the risk of stroke and heart attack by over a third, owning a Zen litter box garden has been proven to add at least nine additional lives to your running total.

Zen emphasizes rigorous self-control and is about looking inward and truly knowing oneself and one's needs. When we forget ourselves, we become one with the environment around us. And that is where we find our garden.

The Zen litter box garden is an example of the isolation of basic elements of ourselves. Here, in its modesty and ease, we encounter

the unexpected. Soft grains are underfoot. Protrusions of rocks poke out from the swirling sands, jarring in their majestic simplicity. Wet clumps of moisture are buried amongst the barren landscape. All of these elements are brought together to give the perfect feel of nature.

A wise Zen master once said, "I stroke my cat. My cat is annoyed. I ignore my cat. My cat loves me. And in time, the cycle repeats itself. My life continues in a wonderfully circular fashion of impermanence." Zen litter box gardening is about embracing this cycle. And perhaps at the end of this journey you'll have a new way of seeing the world, ever more grateful for the colorful balls of yarn that roll your way.

GARDENS AND CATS

I have lived with several Zen masters—all of them cats.

–Eckhart Tolle

The domain of the Zen litter box garden is, traditionally, the cat. Humans have a long relationship with cats going back thousands of years ago when people were already living with cats in their homes and plucking hairballs out of their dinner.

Zen gardens also go back more than 1,000 years in Japan, as places that deliberately compel one to take the time to look around. In these gardens is where one observes the smaller fragments of life around oneself. Where one learns to listen to spirit, and body, and the needs of each. It's a perfect setting for an enlightenment experience.

Here, these coexisting traditions merge in your Zen litter box garden. Just as Zen gardens draw contrasts between the rough and the smooth, the tough and the delicate, cats draw out both the cuddly and the callous, the indifferent and the indebted. At once gleefully chasing a laser pointer and clawing at your leather otto-man. At once settling in the warmth of your lap and pushing a full glass of water off a table.

As the poet Abdal-Hayy Moore says, "We have the chance to glimpse the meaning of the world in a grain of sand, for it has been framed in majestic simplicity." What better way to make good on that chance than in the case of feeling the breeze, playing with kittens, and stepping into your litter box garden?

STEPPING
INSIDE

Entering a garden

forms a kinship

drawing you in

like tasty catnip

—*Ancient Zen Poem*

oes one "keep" a Zen garden litter box? One does, of course, maintain it—raking the granules, redistributing the rocks, moving the cats around. But while it is yours, it is also not yours. You should not be attached, but you should also not be averse. Only when you can be extremely pliable and soft can you be extremely strong. It is this paradox of Zen that will allow you to best experience your litter box garden.

Take your litter box tray and ruminate for a moment. Its simple composition is designed to incite meditation. We often are lost when it comes to dealing with the impermanence of all things and suffering, but our litter box garden affords us a place for it. Think of a cat: walking gracefully, moving mindfully, sauntering with ease from moment to moment. If you find yourself straining, acknowledge the pain and let the moment pass. Allow yourself forgiveness and fluctuation. There may be days where you may only lightly tickle the sand, others when you plunge in deep. Some days you might fully rearrange rocks, some days when you only bat your paws at tiny pebbles. As Zhuangzi says, "Let things take their course. It's all the flow of life, contained in a box."

REACHING ENLIGHTENMENT

Deep within each one of us lies a garden. And in that garden, there's probably a cat snoozing on some rocks.

—Zen Proverb

The immediate impression coming upon a litter box garden is at once soothing and shocking. The findings are there to both disarm and inspire us. It is, ultimately, a place to take off from and a place to come back to; a place to remember how cats can teach us to be mindful. To paraphrase Zhuangzi, the way a cat moves through the world is just as wholly remarkable and unremarkable as enlightenment itself.

Legend tells of a Zen master who lived with a tabby cat in a small flat in Osaka. His cat was his entire

world, and he always brought the cat along to his meditation sessions and classes. When he passed on, his students asked, "What do we do with the cat?" They all decided that in honor of their former master the cat would keep attending their classes. Traveling disciples would observe the cat in class and determine that the cat was due credit for the elimination of negative energy and the increase in concentration in the students. And so, more and more Zen classes began to introduce cats. No one was surprised that all the while the cats simply did nothing, save for the occasional licking of themselves.

Ask yourself what you're assuming to be true in your own life and what you think you need to rely on others to achieve. We all take on so much weight in our day-to-day lives, just letting our negative feelings internalize and pile up and up. Most of all, we don't know how to properly release it, and we don't feel like we can attain that release on our own. Anyone can do it, but so often we hold it in and don't allow ourselves the life, body, and mood-altering experience.

It is our hope that you bring this experience to your Zen garden litter box. Prepare to rid yourself of ills. Slide the black tray out of the box. Pour in the litter, scatter your rocks, position the two cats. Feel how it's at once intimate and remote. Drag the tiny rake across the grains, dig your paws into the sandy clay, nestle yourself into any portion of your garden. Let the weight you carry go, and brace yourself to feel as light and lovely in your life as your feline friends do at the fishmongers.

To quote an ancient Zen master, "In the end, it resides in you. But a cat can help."

This book has been bound using
handcraft methods and
Smyth-sewn to ensure durability.

The text was written by Sarah Royal.

The box and interior were
illustrated by Amber Day.

The box and interior were
designed by Rachel Peckman.